Easy and Delicious Homemade Bread

Beginner's Guide

Jenny Davis

Just to say "thank you" for buying this book, I'd like to give you a gift *absolutely free*

Top Homemade Dip and Spread Recipes

To claim your copy, simply go to:
www.alvobooks.com/diprecipes

First published in 2014 by Alvo Books

Contents

Introduction

Some people imagine that making their own bread at home would be a laborious endeavor, filled with arcane recipes, hard to understand techniques, and intimidating yeast cultures. They weigh these challenges against the convenience of simply walking down the bread aisle of the grocery store, and plucking a loaf from the shelves.

The truth is that making your own bread at home is not that hard at all! In fact, once you understand the ingredients, you'll be surprised to find that the techniques for making delicious bread at home are actually easy to master.

The smell of freshly baked bread wafting through the house is heavenly, as is the amazing feeling slicing into your first loaf while it's still warm, and enjoying the delicious, natural goodness of homemade bread. I guarantee that once you start making your own bread, you'll be hooked.

This book guides you through all of the information and techniques you need to make your own bread. Build your confidence up by starting with the beer bread and cornbread recipes and then move onto yeasted breads. Before you know it, you'll be amazing friends and family with your own sourdough and much more.

Let's get started!

Why make your own bread?

The savings of making your own bread are immense; it's rare for a homemade loaf of bread to cost more than a dollar. Compare that to the prices you find on the shelf in the grocery store and consider the fact that you'll probably go through several loaves of bread each week.

Of course, that store-bought loaf doesn't just come with a higher price tag, it also comes with dough conditioners, additives, preservatives, and a heap of sugar. That loaf is jam-packed with tasty sounding things like calcium propionate, calcium sulfate, and potassium iodate.

All that extra money you're spending isn't just buying you convenience, it's also buying you a handful of strange chemicals you need to look up on the Internet to understand. I would argue that learning how to bloom yeast, knead dough, and bake a tasty loaf at home is much less complicated than figuring out what kind of strange chemicals you're feeding your family every day, wouldn't you?

Understanding flour

Wheat flours

Different types of wheat make different types of flour. Not every kind of flour can make quality bread dough. Protein content is the most influential factor in determining if a type of flour should be used for bread. The protein content of most flours is directly related to the available gluten that flour can create.

Gluten is a large protein molecule that, when hydrated, forms protein chains that tangle together and give dough the structure that holds it together. This structure then captures the gas bubbles created by yeast, steam, or chemical leavening agents that cause the bread to rise.

Cake flour
Cake flour has very low protein content, averaging around 7 to 9 percent. As a result, it has a very low amount of available gluten. While this makes for soft, tender cakes, and pastries, it has little of the structure required for making bread. Cake flour is also treated with chlorine dioxide or chlorine gas to help whiten it. This chemical change makes cake flour more acidic and less hospitable for yeast.

Whole wheat flour
Whole wheat flour has high protein content, averaging between 11 and 15 percent. Unfortunately, not all of this protein is available as gluten. A large amount of the protein in whole wheat flour is locked up in the germ and bran coating that is ground into the flour. While wheat germ and bran contribute

healthy nutrients as well as fiber, they ultimately interfere with gluten formation.

Bread dough made completely from whole wheat flour will not have enough gluten to maintain a significant rise. As a result, unless you like very dense, heavy bread, it can be a good idea to add a little all-purpose or bread flour to whole wheat bread.

All-purpose flour

All-purpose flour has modest protein content averaging between 11 and 12 percent. This amount of available gluten works well with breads that use chemical leavening agents. While all-purpose flour can be used to make a yeast-leavened bread, it doesn't usually have the same rise as dough made from bread flour. It is also worth noting that because all-purpose flour comes from regional blends of ground wheat, the protein content can be inconsistent from one bag of flour to the next.

Bread flour

Bread flour averages between 12 and 13 percent protein content. As a result, it has enough available gluten to make dough that will be sturdy enough to trap the gasses released by yeast.

Self-rising flour

Self-rising flour is actually a blend of all-purpose flour combined with the chemical leavening agent baking powder. It is often used for quick breads and pastries, however, it should not be used for yeast-raised bread dough. Self-rising flour often requires sifting, or whisking, to break up any small clumps before being incorporated with the wet ingredients. Self-rising flour should be stored in a sealed container, and kept in low humidity to prolong the shelf-life of the baking powder.

Gluten-free flours

People who suffer from celiac disease, or who are otherwise intolerant to wheat flours and gluten, need alternative flours to produce bread. Luckily for these people the marketplace is awash with alternative flour blends.

These gluten-free flours are blends of different flours and starches which are then supplemented with xanthan gum. This naturally occurring gum is an emulsifier that can behave like gluten. These specialty blends are all specific to the manufacturer, so you need to read the label closely.

A quick rule of thumb for determining if a gluten-free flour blend can be used for making bread is to look at the grams of protein per quarter cup. All-purpose flour averages 3 grams of protein per quarter. A gluten-free flour blend that has 3 grams of protein per quarter cup should be able to replicate the role of all-purpose flour.

For easy reference, here is a list of flours and starches that are gluten-free:

- Rice flour (including brown rice flour and rice starch)
- Potato starch
- Corn flour, cornmeal and corn starch
- Tapioca flour and starch (tapioca is sometimes also called cassava or manioc)
- Amaranth flour
- Arrowroot
- Millet flour
- Quinoa flour
- Sorghum flour

- Lupin flour
- Buckwheat flour (despite the name, buckwheat has no relation to wheat)
- Almond meal (and other nut flours)
- Coconut flour
- Garbanzo, fava, soy, and other legume flours
- Meals made from chia seeds, flaxseeds, and other seeds

As you can see, there are plenty of options for people needing to avoid gluten!

The art and science of gluten

What is gluten?
Gluten is a large protein molecule found in wheat-based flours. When flour is dry, the gluten molecules are inert and simply slip past each other. When gluten is hydrated by water, these molecules expand and interact with each other. If too little water is used, the amount of available gluten is low; the dough tends to crumble instead of stretch. Too much water dilutes the gluten content of the dough giving you a sticky mass of a dough ball that struggles to hold together.

How does gluten behave?
On a microscopic level a gluten molecule is a long strand which is also a coil that looks like an elongated spring. This means that the gluten molecules can entangle with each other as well as connect end to end. When you stretch a dough ball you are actually stretching millions of microscopic gluten coils. Just like pulling on a spring, it stretches out and then bounces back. However, the bonds between these coils are weak. This means over time the dough goes through a process known as relaxation. Some of the bonds between gluten chains break down allowing the dough to become loose, and thus rise with the gasses released by yeast, steam, or chemical leavening agents.

Relation to salt
Salt is a double-edged sword in its relationship to gluten. All breads need a little salt to maximize flavor. Bread without salt is flat and tastes a bit like cardboard. When dough is being kneaded, salt helps strengthen the tangles of protein chains giving you more structure to hold gas bubbles. However, if salt is added into the dough mixture with the water, it will form a

relationship with the water. As a result there will be less water available to hydrate the gluten and release it from its inert state in the flour.

For bread recipes that require kneading, you will get better gluten formation by reserving the salt at first. Instead, combine all other ingredients, water, yeast, flour, and oil. Then allow the dough to sit for 5 minutes while the flour absorbs the water and hydrates the gluten molecules. The salt can then be added in small increments during the kneading process.

Understanding yeast

Yeast is a naturally occurring fungus, of which there are many different types. The two most common types of yeast used by humans are known as brewer's yeast and baker's yeast. Brewer's yeast should never be used for baking as it is responsible for the production of alcohol!

In bread making, baker's yeast metabolizes the sugars and starches in dough. In the process, the yeast gives off carbon dioxide which is captured by the gluten chains and causes the dough to rise.

Blooming yeast

"Blooming" yeast means to activate it, or bring the fungus to life. You need to do this with some yeasts before you can add them to the flour and other ingredients.

The most simple way to bloom yeast is to add it to a small amount of tepid water with a little sugar. The water should be body temperature or lukewarm – it shouldn't feel either hot or cold to the touch. Once you have the yeast, sugar, and water in a bowl, simply stir and then leave it to sit for 5 to 10 minutes. It should then start bubbling, frothing, and become creamy – your yeast is alive!

The recipes in this book will take you through exactly how to deal with the yeast for each type of bread.

Types of yeast

There are many different types of baker's yeast available to home bakers.

Cake yeast

Cake yeast is not actually yeast for baking cakes. It is active yeast that is wet and has been compressed into a small brick – hence also being called compressed yeast. Cake yeast is one of the original ways bakers kept yeast. Manufacturers have found ways to safely develop cake yeast and sell it in sealed packages. It needs to be bloomed in warm water. It can be hard for the novice baker to work with and keep alive, so, it is best reserved for experienced bakers.

Active dry yeast

Active dry yeast is the most common and easiest yeast for the average home baker. The yeast is dried and kept dormant. You usually see it in little packets in the grocery store, however, with some careful shopping you can buy in bulk or in a vacuum sealed brick. Stored in a jar in the refrigerator, the yeast can stay viable for up to six months, while a vacuum-sealed brick can be kept in the freezer for two years or more.

Active dry yeast needs to be rehydrated and bloomed before you can use it. Simply add the yeast to warm water. Stir to incorporate it, and wait 5 to 7 minutes for the yeast granules to bloom. If the recipe you are using has sugar, you should add it to the water as this will help the yeast bloom a little faster. The yeast is properly bloomed when the water forms a frothy head.

Instant yeast

Instant yeast is a form of active dry yeast. It does not need to be bloomed in water, and can be directly added to the flour. It proofs vigorously for a short period of time, so it cannot be used in any recipes that call for slow proofing or sponges. It has a poor shelf life so it is best to buy it in small quantities.

Rapid-rise yeast

Rapid rise yeast is sometimes also referred to as bread machine yeast. Its biggest advantage is that it blooms and proofs quickly and vigorously. It contributes very little flavor to the bread dough and makes small bubbles that can sometimes give the bread a spongy texture. Rapid rise yeast suffers from the same short shelf life as instant yeast.

Chemical leavening agents

How do they work?
In yeast-risen bread the firm gluten structure of the dough holds the gas bubbles produced by the yeast. Some bread is made from mixtures that are wetter. This classifies them as batter instead of dough. Batter does a poor job of holding slow developing gas bubbles. Batter based breads, like biscuits and corn bread, require fast chemical leavening that relies on reactions between acidic and alkaline compounds.

Baking powder
Baking powder is a balanced leavening agent. It is made up of crystalized acid and alkaline compounds, along with some starch to stabilize it. When introduced to water, the crystals dissolve and begin to react with each other creating carbon dioxide bubbles. Because the reaction of these two compounds is often shorter than the baking time, most batter based breads often require the assistance of another chemical leavening agent.

Baking soda
Baking soda – or sodium bicarbonate – is a purely alkaline compound that requires an acidic liquid to activate it. This reaction happens based on the balance between the acidic liquid both in strength and proportion. If the proportion is wrong then some of the additional compound will remain in the final product, altering the flavor. In the case of buttermilk biscuits, ½ teaspoon of baking soda will be neutralized by the acid in 1 cup of buttermilk.

Bread-making techniques

What is kneading?

Kneading is essential for bread dough that is leavened by yeast. By folding the dough over in successive layers you increase the density of the tangled protein chains. The more these protein chains tangle together, the more gas they will be able to retain from the active yeast, and as a result you will get a better rise during the proofing stage.

Often times when people think of kneading dough they picture a kindly old grandmother rocking her hands back in forth in a massive dough ball. While this technically is kneading, and will indeed increase the number of tangled protein chains, it is not the best technique you can use.

How to knead

The best technique for kneading begins by spreading the dough out on a lightly floured work surface and folding it over on itself. Each time, before you fold, you should sprinkle a little salt on half of the dough. This way when you fold it, the salt is now buried in the center of the dough, where it can form a stronger relationship with the gluten chains.

I find it is best to think of the folding technique in terms of the compass rose. You sprinkle a little salt on the east half of the dough, then fold the west half over top of it. Press down firmly to spread the dough out flat. Then sprinkle salt on the south half of the dough, before folding the north half over top of it and press it flat. This process is repeated until all of the salt is incorporated into the dough.

The act of folding the dough over itself increases the density of the tangled protein chains better than simply manipulating the dough ball randomly with your hands.

Eventually enough gluten chains will form in the dough and it will start to resist folding. At this point you can begin rocking it back and forth or simply massaging it in your hands. In general, it will require 8 to 10 minutes of kneading by hand. If you are using a dough hook in a stand mixer, the dough will climb the hook after 7 or 8 minutes indicating that it is sufficiently kneaded.

If you are not sure whether the dough has been sufficiently kneaded, you can pull off a golf-ball-sized piece and stretch it into a thin sheet. The sheet should be thin enough that if you hold it up to a light you can see the light glow throw. If the gluten chains are strong enough, the dough will stretch without breaking. If it breaks continue kneading.

Proofing

Proofing is the process by which the gasses given off by active yeast cause the dough to rise. The gas suspended in the dough causes it to increase in volume as well as develop flavor.

After your dough has been properly kneaded, you have several options for proofing. These options are going to be influenced by the type of yeast you are using as well as the type of bread you are making. Yeast reproduces faster at warm temperatures. The ideal location is an oven that has been warmed to 90 to 100 degrees Fahrenheit. Be mindful that yeast dies at 140 degrees, so make sure the oven isn't too hot!

If you live in a warm climate, you can simply leave your bread to proof anywhere that's draft-free. Leaving it in the microwave or oven – turned off – are sure options, but if you have a corner or nook where it won't be disturbed, that's fine too.

There are some types of bread, such as ciabatta, that call for slow proofing. Letting the dough sit out in a covered bowl at room temperature for up to a day allows the yeast to contribute a lot of flavor to the dough. The recipes in this book all explain the proofing techniques for each specific recipe.

When the dough has proofed long enough to double in volume, it is time to punch it down and begin forming the loaf. Once you have formed the loaf, there will be a second, shorter proofing period where the dough rises again to the size desired for baking.

Forming loaves

Once your dough has proofed and risen to double its original volume, it is time to punch it down and form the loaf shape you choose. The term "punching down" is somewhat of a misnomer. What you are really doing is gently suggesting it into a dough ball that can be shaped to the loaf style of your choice.

Types of loaves
Many bread recipes call for their own style and shape of loaf.

The classic sandwich loaf calls for the dough ball to be flattened into a rectangle and rolled into a length that matches a 9 inch loaf pan. It is then placed into the loaf pan and put back in the oven to proof again to rise again to its final volume.

If you prefer to make buns, you would roll the dough ball out into a tube. Use a board scraper to cut the tube in half, then cut those halves into quarters for large buns or cut the quarters into eighths for small buns.

Some more rustic types of bread are simply shaped with the hands into a rough oval or circle and then baked on a tray.

These are just general guidelines for forming loaves for basic bread. The special recipes to follow will discuss how each particular loaf is formed.

Once you have the loaf shape you prefer, you should lightly dampen the surface of the dough by running a wet hand over it. Then take a knife and score the top of the bread with either a single slash down the middle or three diagonal slashes.

Bread is baked at different times and temperatures depending on the type of bread, the type of pan, and the shape of the loaf. All breads should be baked to an internal temperature of 200 degrees Fahrenheit. You can check the temperature with a basic probe thermometer inserted into the side or bottom of the loaf. Unless the pan you are using prevents it, you should avoid inserting the thermometer into the top of the loaf as it will release the bread's internal steam, potentially collapsing the crust.

The role of steam
Steam is an important element in baking yeast-raised bread. If a formed loaf is allowed to dry out on top during the final proof, it will limit the final volume. The gas bubbles in the dough expand early in the baking process. If the loaf has a soft top from the presence of steam, this added lift can expand it by up to 10 percent.

Later in the baking process as the crust is starting to form, the presence of steam will aid in browning and make the crust thicker.

Many bakers develop their own method for providing steam in the oven. Opening the oven periodically and using a spray bottle, pointed up and away from the heating element, is a common method. A shallow pan of water placed in the oven away from the main loaf is an easy option that doesn't require you to open the oven door, which can cause problems because it lets the heat out.

Equipment

Bread machines

The world of bread making has exploded in recent years with a plethora of bread making machines. While each manufacturer has their own recipe and procedures for their particular machine, they all essentially based on the same core idea. You add ingredients to the machine as per the instructions, and a few minutes later a wad of dough is ready to be formed into a loaf.

The bread you get in the end product will indeed be serviceable. When you bake it, the bread will give off that characteristic toasted wheat smell that fills the house with memories of visits to grandma's. It will be free of the additives and dough conditioners of store bought bread.

However, at the end of the day, dough made from a bread machine tends to lack character. Most bread machines use rapid rise yeast, which leaves little time for flavor to develop. Rapid rise yeast also has a tendency to make bread that has a soft and spongy texture.

The biggest problem with bread machines is that you get what you pay for. This means to get a good one you are going to have to invest a serious amount of money. Most quality bread machines are over two hundred U.S. dollars. A few of the high-end bread machines can cost over five hundred U.S. dollars.

This means a bread machine will take a long time to pay for itself. You lose most of the cost savings benefits that come from baking your own bread to buy a machine that essentially has only one function in the household.

Stand mixers

Most households have stand mixers, and most stand mixers come with multiple attachments. While a quality stand mixer is around the same price as a bread machine, the stand mixer is a multitasking appliance. You can use it for cookies, cakes, and pies. It can whip cream, stir batter, and some attachments even allow you to roll out pasta and grind meat. Even though you spend the same amount of money, the stand mixer pays for itself sooner because it can do so many other things in the kitchen.

One of the most common attachments for a stand mixer is the dough hook. A dough hook is a thick metal hook that attaches to the stand mixer's planetary assembly. You add the ingredients to the locking work bowl and start the mixer on a slow setting until the flour completely incorporates. The dough hook will move the dough around in the work bowl mixing, effectively kneading it.

Eventually enough gluten structure forms in the dough to hold it firmly to the hook. It then begins to climb the hook, and you know it is ready for proofing. Simply remove the hook from the machine and carefully separate the hook from the dough. Return the dough to the work bowl, cover it, and allow it to proof until it doubles in volume.

Upfront cost aside, there are only two drawbacks to using a stand mixer to make bread. The first drawback is the noise. Even the highest quality stand mixer is still loud. The second drawback is that since you have to add the salt at the beginning of the process. The gluten structure formed by dough hook kneading is a little less than if you added the salt in small batches while kneading by hand.

The end result is a slightly longer proofing time and a little less rise in the final loaf. Admittedly, these are minor drawbacks. If you are preparing a single loaf I would still advocate kneading by hand. If you had to bake multiple loaves in a day it is probably more efficient to use the dough hook attachment of a stand mixer.

Loaf pans

While there are many interpretations of the loaf pan, the general standard is a metal pan that is 9 inches long, 5 inches wide, and 3 inches deep. Glass and Pyrex loaf pans are gaining in popularity.

While the materials do not affect the crown of the bread, they do influence the body of the loaf. Metal loaf pans tend to make a crispier crust on the body of the loaf, while glass creates a softer, more tender crust on the lower portion of the loaf. This is due to the fact that metal conducts heat faster, and thus cooks the water vapor out of the lower crust faster.

Usually this is just a matter of taste. People who don't like the crust on a sandwich tend to prefer homemade bread from a glass pan. However, this softer bottom means it takes longer for the crust to set after it is turned out from the pan. Since a metal loaf pan has a firmer lower crust, you can cut into it sooner without crushing the loaf.

People who want to cut into the loaf quickly to see butter melt into a warm slice of bread will probably prefer a metal loaf pan.

Pizza stones

These tend to be stone composites in a round shape. Pizza stones mimic the attributes of a classic Italian wood fired pizza oven better than mental trays. Pizza stones are also used for breads that need high heat.

Whenever possible, a pizza stone should be placed in a preheated oven for 10 to 15 minutes before the bread or pizza is put on it. This will allow the stone to build a heat load which can quickly transfer to the loaf, giving it a crispy bottom.

The easiest way to transfer breads directly to a pizza stone is to first assemble them on a sheet of parchment paper that has been laid down on a pizza peel or wooden cutting board.

Once the bread has been assembled on the parchment paper, you can simply open the oven door, bring the cutting board to the pizza stone, and slide the bread from the cutting board to the stone by pulling the parchment paper over.

A pizza stone should always be allowed to cool down in the oven. A hot stone should never be exposed to water as thermal shock and injury could result.

Parchment paper

Parchment paper is a type of paper especially created for baking. It can withstand high temperatures and even bread made from very sticky dough will slide right off after baking.

A good way to save money on parchment paper is to buy it in large rolls. Since it can be used for many other baked goods, such as cookies, it pays for itself faster by serving other roles.

Kneading surfaces

If you don't have a butcher block counter top, a large wooden cutting board is convenient for hand kneading. Bread dough loves to be kneaded on a lightly floured wood surface. The texture of the wood surface tends to give the dough just enough to stick to, while still being able to pull it away. Also, being able to remove the cutting board after kneading speeds clean-up.

Beginner's bread recipes

Beer bread

Beer bread is a form of quick bread, so-called because it's quick and easy to make. If you're a beginner, this is a great type of bread to try.

Beer bread is often made using self-rising flour or chemical leavening agents, combined with beer.

The beer is used to flavor the bread and also serves as the primary liquid. Which beer you choose makes a big difference. Cheap beer from a can will make bread that pales in flavor compared to one made with a craft beer from a glass bottle. Be sure to check the date the beer was bottled, as old beer tends to have a skunk-like flavor that will linger in the bread.

Here are two recipes for beer bread. Please note the way the melted butter is used differently in each recipe.

Lager-style beer bread recipe

Lager is a light, golden beer with a crisp flavor profile. Whenever possible, you should try to source a micro-brewed, or craft-brewed lager. A craft-brewed lager that still has some yeast sediment in the bottom of the bottle will give the bread a mild yeast flavor that most people appreciate.

Equipment
Flour sifter
Large work bowl
Silicone spatula
Standard loaf pan

Ingredients
3 cups of self-rising flour
1 teaspoon of salt
¼ cup of sugar
12 ounce bottle of lager-style beer
4 tablespoons of melted butter
2 tablespoons of cold butter

Method
1. Preheat the oven to 400 degrees Fahrenheit.

2. Sift the self-rising flour into a large work bowl along with the sugar and salt.

3. Grease a standard loaf pan with the cold butter.

4. Using the muffin method, slowly pour the beer onto the dry ingredients.

5. Stir to combine with a silicone spatula.

6. Pour the batter into the greased loaf pan.

7. Pour the melted butter on top but do not stir it in. This will give the beer bread a firm and crispy crust.

8. Place the loaf pan in the middle of the oven rack and bake for 45 to 50 minutes, or until the top of the bread is golden brown and crunchy. Test for an internal temperature of 200 degrees Fahrenheit.

The butter being poured on top of the loaf gives it a crispy and flavorful crust. If you find the first time you make this beer bread that the interior feels a little too dry and crumbly for your taste, simply mix half of the melted butter into the batter during step 5.

Nutrition facts
Serving size: 1 slice
Servings per pan: 12
Calories: 158
Fat: 4g
Sodium: 198mg
Total Carbs: 26.5g
Fiber: 1g
Protein: 3g

Stout-style beer bread recipe

Equipment
Flour sifter
Large work bowl
Medium work bowl
Silicone spatula
Standard loaf pan

Ingredients
3 cups of self-rising flour
1 teaspoon of salt
3 tablespoons of malted barley syrup
12 ounce bottle of stout-style beer
4 tablespoons of melted butter
2 tablespoons of cold butter

Method
1. Preheat the oven to 400 degrees Fahrenheit.

2. Sift the self-rising flour into a large work bowl along with the salt.

3. Grease a standard loaf pan with the cold butter.

4. Slowly pour the beer into a small bowl with the malted barley syrup. Stir to combine.

5. Using the muffin method, slowly pour the beer and malted barley syrup onto the dry ingredients.

6. Pour the melted butter into the mixture, and stir to combine with a silicone spatula. This will give the entire bread a softer texture.

7. Pour the batter into the greased loaf pan.

8. Place the loaf pan in the middle of the oven rack and bake for 45 to 50 minutes, or until the top of the bread is golden brown and crunchy. Test for an internal temperature of 200 degrees Fahrenheit.

The malted barley syrup in this recipe really heightens the toasted and sweet flavors of the stout-style beer. The butter being incorporated into the mixture creates a softer texture, but less of a crispy thick crust.

Nutrition facts
Serving size: 1 slice
Servings per pan: 12
Calories: 158
Fat: 4g
Sodium: 202mg
Total Carbs: 26g
Fiber: 1g
Protein: 4g

Corn bread

Traveling across the United States you will find a myriad of corn bread variations. Home cooks and restaurateurs often make their own minor tweaks to this beloved staple. In northern states corn bread tends to be a little sweeter, and has an almost cake-like consistency. In the South corn bread traditionally has a lighter texture, a savory flavor profile, and a thicker crust. The thick crust in southern-style corn bread is usually a result of baking it in a seasoned cast iron pan.

In the grocery store you can often buy a box mix or corn bread kit. You simply add water, stir to combine, and pour the mixture into a greased baking pan bound for the oven. While this will give you a cake similar to northern-style corn bread it often lacks the depth of flavor that you can only get from using real corn.

Obviously sweet corn picked fresh in-season and cut from the cob will give you the most corn flavor. If you have access to a local farmer's market you can try unique varieties that will give the batter even more character. Country Gentleman, Bodacious, Texas Honey June, and Jubilee are varieties that improve both the flavor and the texture of the corn bread.

Unfortunately, fresh corn is only in season for a few months out of the year. Your options for the rest of the year essentially boil down to canned whole kernel corn, canned cream corn or flash frozen corn.

Cream corn is simply too wet and too sweet. Using it for corn bread will create a thick, corn cake that only vaguely resembles a northern-style corn bread. Canned whole kernel corn processes quickly and incorporates easily into the mixture. Unfortunately, it is full of salt and other preservatives, and most of the flavor has been leached out in the canning process.

The best option when fresh corn is out of season is to use flash frozen, whole kernel corn. The flash freezing process preserves the flavor while the kernels only require a modest amount of processing. If corn is out of season and you are using frozen corn, be sure to give the kernels at least a half hour to thaw ahead of time.

Here are two recipes for corn bread, one northern-style corn bread and one southern-style.

Northern-style corn bread

Equipment
Food processor
Large work bowl
Silicone spatula
8 inch square Pyrex baking dish

Ingredients
1¼ cups of yellow cornmeal
1¼ cups of all-purpose flour
1 cup of whole kernel corn
1 teaspoon of salt
2 teaspoons of baking powder
¼ teaspoon of baking soda
1 cup of buttermilk
¼ cup of brown sugar
2 eggs
8 tablespoons of butter, melted
1 tablespoon of cold butter

Method
1. Preheat the oven to 425 degrees Fahrenheit.

2. Grease the baking dish with the tablespoon of cold butter.

3. Combine the cornmeal, flour, salt, baking powder, and baking soda in a large work bowl.

4. Pour the buttermilk, brown sugar, corn, and eggs into a food processor. Pulse the food processor 5 to 7 times to break down the corn and combine the ingredients.

5. It is best to combine the two mixtures using the muffin method. Slowly pour the wet mixture onto the dry ingredients in the work bowl. Fold the wet mixture into the dry with a silicone spatula.

6. Use the muffin method, pour the melted butter onto the batter and stir to combine.

7. Pour the batter into the greased Pyrex baking pan. Shake the pan back and forth a few times to level the batter out. Then smooth the top with the spatula.

8. Place the pan in the oven and bake for 30 minutes or until a tooth pick can be inserted into the center and comes out clean.

9. Take the pan out of the oven and allow it to cool for 15 minutes before turning it over onto a wooden cutting board.

10. Cut the corn bread into squares using a serrated bread knife. Plate each piece right side up.

Northern-style corn bread is best served warm. You can wrap leftovers in plastic and keep in the refrigerator overnight. Reheat the next day in an oven that has been preheated to 350 degrees Fahrenheit for 10 minutes.

Nutrition facts
Serving size: One 4″ by 4″ square
Servings per pan: 4
Calories: 439.7
Fat: 5.1g
Sodium: 673.6mg

Total Carbs: 111.7g
Fiber: 12.5g
Protein: 13.8g

Southern-style corn bread

This style of corn bread has a savory flavor profile and a lighter texture than northern-style corn bread. One of the hallmark aspects of southern-style corn bread is the crispy crust it gets from being baked at high heat in a preheated cast iron pan. If you don't have a cast iron pan you can use a 9 inch square Pyrex baking pan, but it will not give you the same crisp crust.

The pan is traditionally greased with rendered bacon fat. If you don't have bacon fat available use melted vegetable shortening. Butter is not an advised substitute unless you have clarified the butter to remove the trace water content.

Equipment
Food processor
Large work bowl
Silicone spatula
9 inch cast iron pan

Ingredients
2 tablespoons of bacon drippings
1 cup of yellow cornmeal
¼ cup of all-purpose flour
1 teaspoon of sugar
½ cup of whole kernel corn
1 teaspoon of sugar
1 teaspoon of baking powder
½ teaspoon of baking soda
1 teaspoon of salt
1 cup of buttermilk
1 large egg, beaten

Method

1. Place the dry cast iron pan in an oven that has been preheated to 450 degrees Fahrenheit. It is best to have the oven rack in the lower middle, and make sure it pulls out easily for when you pour the batter into the pan. The cast iron pan needs a minimum of 15 minutes to heat up.

2. Combine the cornmeal and salt in a large work bowl.

3. Pour the buttermilk, sugar, corn, and egg into a food processor. Pulse the food processor 5 to 7 times to combine.

4. Slowly pour the wet mixture from the food processor into the work bowl with the cornmeal. Stir to combine. Allow the batter to sit undisturbed for five minutes. This will help the cornmeal to properly hydrate, which will give you a lighter, softer corn bread.

5. Add the flour, baking soda, and baking powder to the work bowl. Fold the mixture together with a silicone spatula.

6. Once the cast iron pan is very hot, slide the rack out of the oven enough that you have full access to the pan.

7. Pour the bacon fat into the pan. Use the silicone spatula to make sure the bottom is thoroughly greased.

8. Pour the mixture into the pan.

9. Bake for 20 minutes or until the top is golden brown and a tooth pick can be inserted into the middle and comes out clean.

10. Turn the corn bread out onto a wooden cutting board. Then return the cast iron pan to the oven to slowly cool down. Do not place the cast iron pan in the sink when it is still hot. Exposure to water could potentially cause thermal shock, damaging the pan, or causing injury.

11. Allow the corn bread to cool for five minutes before cutting and serving.

Southern-style corn bread does not keep well when left over. However you can wrap leftovers in foil and keep in the refrigerator overnight. Reheat the next day in an oven that has been preheated to 350 degrees Fahrenheit for 10 minutes.

Nutrition facts
Serving size: 1 slice
Servings per pan: 8
Calories: 126
Fat: 7.3g
Sodium: 112mg
Total Carbs: 18g
Fiber: 1.4g
Protein: 3.6g

Buttermilk biscuits

Classic buttermilk biscuits are a staple at many kitchen tables across the United States. It is admittedly easy to make a pedestrian wad of a biscuit and hide it under rich sawmill gravy. However, creating a biscuit that is flavorful as well as tender and flaky requires precision, as well as an understanding of two important principles.

The first of these two principles is the balance required in the relationship between leavening agents and acids. In this recipe we are talking about the relationship between baking soda, baking powder, and the acidic nature of buttermilk.

The second principle at play in making quality buttermilk biscuits is the texture that is produced by the fats. Butter is 20 percent water, and the temperature at which that water integrates with the flour as well as the timing of when the fats melt will do much to determine the texture of the biscuit when baked.

Using softened or melted butter will create a firm crisp biscuit. To get a tender yet flaky batch of biscuits it is better to use frozen butter that has been grated through a standard box grater shortly before mixing.

Equipment
Box grater
Small work bowl
Large work bowl
Measuring cups
Baking sheet
Rolling pin

Biscuit cutter (or a metal measuring cup)
Fork
Basting brush

Ingredients
8 tablespoons of butter, frozen
2 tablespoons of butter, melted
2 cups of all-purpose flour
1 tablespoon of baking powder
½ teaspoon of baking soda
1 cup of buttermilk
1 teaspoon of sugar
½ teaspoon of salt

Method
1. Two hours before baking, open a stick of butter and place it in the freezer along with a dinner fork. Make sure the buttermilk is thoroughly chilled in the refrigerator as well.

2. Preheat the oven to 425 degrees Fahrenheit.

3. Grate the frozen butter through a box grater into a small work bowl. Place the bowl back in the freezer to keep the butter cold.

4. Combine the dry ingredients. Place the flour, sugar, salt, baking powder, and baking soda in a large bowl.

5. Add the grated butter to the dry ingredients, and press it into the dry mixture with the chilled dinner fork. The pieces of butter should be the size of a large grain of rice.

6. Pour the buttermilk over the dry mixture. Stir briskly for one minute, or until the batter just comes together. It should not be

completely smooth. Instead it should look more like cooked oatmeal.

7. Dust your counter with flour and pour the batter over the top of it. Collect the mass of batter together and lightly press it into a rectangle.

8. Fold the left hand side of the rectangle into the middle. Then fold the right hand side of the rectangle over the top of the first two layers. Press the layers together with the palm of your hand.

9. Use a rolling pin to roll the dough into a ¾ inch thickness.

10. Using a large biscuit cutter, or a 1 cup size metal measuring cup, press down into the dough to cut a round biscuit section. You want as little space between cuts as possible so you don't waste any dough.

11. Place the biscuits on an ungreased baking sheet. The biscuits should all be touching. This contact will help them rise together.

12. Use the basting brush to paint the top of the biscuits with melted butter.

13. Bake for 12 to 15 minutes or until plump and golden-brown.

14. Remove the biscuits from the oven, and allow them to cool for 3 to 5 minutes before serving. They should be just cool enough to be pulled apart, yet warm enough to instantly melt butter spread on them.

Buttermilk biscuits are best served and consumed as fresh as possible. If you do have some biscuits leftover, you can wrap them in foil and keep them in the refrigerator overnight. Reheat them by placing them in an oven that has been preheated to 350 degrees Fahrenheit, for 5 minutes.

Nutrition facts
Serving size: 1 biscuit
Servings per batch: 8
Calories: 232
Fat: 11.6g
Sodium: 161 mg
Total Carbs: 27.6g
Fiber: 1g
Protein: 4.25g

Popovers

Popovers are a savory American take on the British Yorkshire pudding and the French *pâte à choux*, or Choux pastry.

The characteristic rise is caused by steam generated by the liquids in the batter, which is cooked at a high heat. The temperature of the ingredients is critical in giving popovers their lift. When the ingredients are warmed before mixing, the exterior of the batter sets quickly in the oven. This allows steam to be trapped inside and expand into an amorphous bread bubble.

In this recipe you want to have the eggs at room temperature, the butter melted, and the milk warmed before starting. While you can make popovers in a muffin tin, you will get a larger crown due to better steam expansion if you spend the extra money to buy a popover pan.

Please note that once these go in the oven, the door is not to be opened until the time is up. The delicate structure inside is based on the constant pressure of the steam. Opening the door releases some of the heat and the temperature won't be able to bounce back fast enough to keep the crown from falling. You've been warned – don't open the oven!

Popover recipe

Equipment
Microwave safe measuring cup
Blender
Popover pan or muffin tin

Ingredients
1½ cups of all-purpose flour
1½ cups of whole milk, warmed
¾ teaspoon of salt
3 large eggs, at room temperature
2 tablespoons of unsalted butter

Method
1. Preheat the oven to 400 degrees Farenheit.

2. Put the milk and butter into a microwave safe measuring cup. Microwave for 2 minutes, or until the milk is warm to the touch and the butter is melted.

3. Spray each of the popover cups with non-stick cooking spray.

4. Pour the milk and butter into a blender with the salt and eggs. Blend on a high setting to combine.

5. Add the flour to the mixture, and run the blender on a high setting for two minutes, or until the batter is smooth, yet full of little bubbles.

6. Quickly pour the batter equally into the six cups of the popover pan.

7. Place it immediately in the preheated oven.

8. Bake undisturbed for 40 minutes.

9. When the popovers come out of the oven, immediately turn them out onto a wooden cutting board. Use a paring knife to make a small slit in the top of each one to let the steam out. Serve immediately.

Popovers are best served with a honey butter spread made of 1 tablespoon of honey whipped with 4 tablespoons of butter. Popovers are a great substitute for dinner rolls, but they do not keep well as leftovers.

Nutrition facts
Serving size: 1 popover
Servings per pan: 6
Calories: 209.5
Fat: 8.5g
Sodium: 351mg
Total Carbs: 25.5g
Fiber: 1g
Protein: 8g

Flatbread

Traditionally flatbreads are a family of bread that is completely unleavened by yeast, steam or chemical leavening agents. One popular exception to this is pita bread, which uses yeast for leavening. A basic flatbread is made with all-purpose flour, water, and salt. However, since it is such a blank canvas, it invites variation. The addition of minced garlic, herbs, olive oil, fresh cracked black pepper, and even sun-dried tomatoes really punch up the flavor.

Basic flatbread recipe

This is perhaps one of the easiest recipes for flatbread. This flatbread is intended to be used as a substitute for a dinner roll, or for tearing off and dipping in humus or mopping up sauce.

Equipment
Large work bowl
Plastic mixing spoon
Board scraper
Rolling pin
2 half sheet pans
Parchment paper

Ingredients
2 cups of all-purpose flour
¾ cup of water
½ teaspoon of salt
½ teaspoon of black pepper
1 tablespoon of olive oil

Method

1. Preheat the oven to 400 degrees Fahrenheit.

2. Add the flour, pepper, olive oil, and water to a large work bowl. Stir to combine until the dough is flaky and a little dry to the touch. Dust the dough with additional flour if it feels pasty to the touch.

3. Lightly flour a work surface and knead the dough using the folding technique.

4. Form the dough into a long rectangle and roll it out into a long log shape, 6 to 8 inches long. Cut the log in half with a board scraper. Then cut the halves into quarters.

5. Use a rolling pin to roll the dough ball. Roll it north to south, then east to west and repeat again. This will help the dough keep a relatively round shape. The thinner you roll the dough balls out, the crispier the flatbread will be.

6. Line both half sheet pans with parchment paper.

7. Lay the rolled out dough onto the half sheet pans. You should be able to get two per pan.

8. Place the pans in the oven on separate racks.

9. After 5 minutes check the flatbreads. They should be slightly golden brown on top. The time may vary depending on how thin you rolled them out. The thinner the dough is, the faster it will bake.

10. Use a pancake turner to flip each flatbread. Then switch the pans so the pan that was on the lower rack is now on the upper rack of the oven.

11. Allow them to bake for 5 more minutes.

12. Remove the pans from the oven and stack the flatbreads on top of each other ready to serve.

If you are going to be making multiple batches, you can help keep the first batch of flatbreads warm by covering with tin foil and a tea towel.

Nutrition facts
Serving size: 1 flatbread
Servings per batch: 4
Calories: 152
Fat: 0.5g
Sodium: 164mg
Total Carbs: 32g
Fiber: 1.5g
Protein: 4.5g

Grilled tomato and garlic flatbread

This flatbread is a good appetizer or side dish, especially for Italian meals – it is the perfect companion for a traditional Tuscan white bean soup.

Equipment
Large work bowl
Plastic mixing spoon
Board scraper
Rolling pin
Charcoal or propane grill
Basting brush

Ingredients
2 cups of all-purpose flour
¾ cup of water
½ teaspoon of salt
½ teaspoon of black pepper
4 cloves of garlic, minced
¼ cup of sun-dried tomatoes, minced
4 leaves of basil, chopped fine
1 tablespoon of olive oil
4 tablespoons of olive oil, reserved

Method
1. Preheat your charcoal or propane grill to 350 degrees Fahrenheit.

2. Mince 4 cloves of garlic, the sun-dried tomatoes, and the basil leaves.

3. Add the garlic, tomatoes, and basil to the flour in a large work bowl. Then whisk them together to distribute evenly.

4. Add the pepper, olive oil, and water to the work bowl. Stir to combine until the dough is flaky and a little dry to the touch. Dust the dough with additional flour if it feels pasty to the touch.

5. Lightly flour a work surface and knead the dough using the folding technique. Sprinkle a little bit of salt with each fold until the salt is gone.

6. Form the dough into a long rectangle, and then roll it into a 6 to 8 inch long log shape. Cut the log in half with a board scraper. Then cut the halves into quarters.

7. Use a rolling pin to roll the dough ball. Roll it north to south, then east to west, and repeat again. This will help the dough keep a relatively round shape. The thinner you roll the dough balls out, the crispier the flatbread will be. Because you will be grilling this flatbread I wouldn't advice rolling it thinner than 1/8 of an inch.

8. Use a basting brush to lightly paint the top of each rolled-out dough ball. When you bring the dough to the grill, this will help keep the flatbread from sticking.

9. Make sure you have the reserved olive oil and the basting brush on hand near the grill.

10. Lay the dough directly over the fire with the olive oil painted side facing down. If your grill is small, you may have to grill them in batches.

11. Check the dough after 3 minutes. The bottom should be firm and crisp. The time may vary depending on how thin you rolled them out. The thinner the dough is, the faster it will bake.

12. Use the basting brush to very quickly paint the top with olive oil.

13. Use a pancake turner to flip each flatbread.

14. Allow them to grill for 2 more minutes or until both sides are crisp and show a little char.

15. Remove the flatbread from the grill and stack them on top of each other ready to serve.

If you are going to be making multiple batches, you can help keep the first batch of flatbread warm by covering it with tin foil and a tea towel.

Nutrition facts
Serving size: 1 flatbread
Servings per batch: 4
Calories: 212
Fat: 4.5g
Sodium: 238mg
Total Carbs: 39.5g
Fiber: 3.1g
Protein: 6.2g

Yeast-risen recipes

Basic bread recipe

This is a recipe for a classic white bread loaf. This is the bread you smelled walking into your grandmother's kitchen. While it is a cliché, it is also a practical lesson in baking yeast-raised bread. The principles used in preparing this simple recipe will carry over into most other yeast bread recipes.

While you might have a bread machine or a stand mixer with a dough hook, I personally recommend making this recipe with your own two hands. The authentic experience of doing this the old fashioned way will translate to all the other recipes you are sure to try in this homemade bread book.

As we discussed in the section on understanding flour, bread flour has more gluten and makes a better choice than all-purpose flour. A higher amount of gluten allows the bread to capture and hold more of the gasses given off by the yeast.

Equipment
Microwave safe measuring cup
Wooden cutting board
Large work bowl, with cover or plastic wrap
Plastic mixing spoon
Non-stick cooking spray
Standard loaf pan
Board scraper

Ingredients
1 teaspoon of salt

1¼ cups of warm water (approximately 90 degrees Fahrenheit)
1 tablespoon of sugar
2 tablespoons of olive oil
2 teaspoons of active dry yeast
3 cups of bread flour

Method

1. Pour the water and sugar into a microwave safe mixing cup. Microwave on high for one minute, or until the water reaches a temperature of 90 to 100 degrees Fahrenheit.

2. Stir the water to make sure the sugar has dissolved. Then add the yeast and stir until all the granules have dissolved into the water. Set the cup aside for five minutes to allow the yeast to activate and bloom.

3. Add the flour to a large work bowl.

4. Once the yeast has bloomed and formed a frothy head, pour it onto the flour along with the olive oil. Do not add the salt yet!

5. Stir to combine, and then wait five minutes. This additional time will allow the flour to hydrate, and you will have more gluten available when you knead the dough.

6. Lightly flour a wooden work surface and turn the dough out. Spray the work bowl with non-stick cooking spray.

7. Begin kneading using the folding technique. Press the dough out into a roughly rectangular shape. Sprinkle a little bit of salt on the east side. Fold the west side over it and press it out into a rectangle. Next, sprinkle a little bit of the salt on the south side of the dough and fold the north side over it. Press it out into a

rectangle. Continue folding and sprinkling salt until all of the salt has been used.

Eventually enough gluten chains will form in the dough that it resists folding. At this point you can begin rocking it back and forth, or simply massaging it in your hands. In general, it will require 8 to 10 minutes of kneading by hand. If you are using a dough hook in a stand mixer, the dough will climb the hook after 7 or 8 minutes, indicating that it has been kneaded sufficiently.

If you are not sure whether the dough has been sufficiently kneaded you can pull off a golf-ball-sized piece, and stretch it into a thin sheet. The sheet should be thin enough so that if you hold it up to a light, you can see the light glow through. If the gluten chains are strong enough, the dough will stretch without breaking. If it tears, continue kneading.

8. Once it is sufficiently kneaded, return it to the work bowl. Set your oven to warm for a few minutes. Then wet your hands and rub the surface to wet the dough ball. Cover and place in the warm oven to let the dough proof.

When proofing the internal temperature of the oven should be around 90 to100 degrees Fahrenheit, and never over 120. Allow the dough to rise in the warm oven until it doubles in size. This generally takes around 45 minutes to an hour.

9. This stage is called punching down the dough. Really, you are coaxing it into the shape of a dough ball so you can form the loaf. While this recipe can make two medium sized loaves, it is arguably better to make one large one.

Turn the dough out onto the counter. Using a board scraper, fold the sides under the main mass of the dough. Lift the mass of the dough ball up and pinch the seams together to form a tight dough ball.

10. Use the non-stick cooking spray to grease the loaf pan. Rewarm the oven again if it needs it.

11. Form the final loaf by rolling the dough back and forth evenly until it is the length of the bread pan. When it is the right size, place it in the pan.

12. Wet your hands and lightly rub the loaf just enough to dampen the surface. This will help develop a deeper brown crust. Use a paring knife to make two shallow slits running the long way across the top of the loaf. This will allow the crown to expand fully as the loaf makes its final rise.

13. Place the loaf pan back in the warm oven for the final rise. This will take roughly 30 to 45 minutes. Once the loaf rises an inch or two above the lip of the loaf pan, it is ready to bake. Allowing it to proof longer will give you a larger loaf with a fluffy interior. However, if you allow the loaf to proof too much, the gluten structure of the unbaked crown could fail, and the loaf could potentially collapse.

14. Consider your method for adding steam to the oven. Spraying water from a spray bottle is a common method. However, a small, shallow pan of water placed in the back corner on a lower rack is also an easy option, as you won't lose heat opening the oven door.

15. Bake at 380 degrees Fahrenheit for 30 to 35 minutes, or until the internal temperature of the loaf is 200 degrees Fahrenheit.

16. When the loaf has reached a temperature of 200 degrees Fahrenheit, remove it from the oven. Turn it out of the pan onto a wooden cutting board. You should give the loaf a full hour to cool down. This cooling time will help the crust to set and the internal steam to redistribute. The end result is a loaf that is much easier to cut.

Of course, if you can't resist trying it sooner, no-one will ever know!

Nutrition facts
Serving size: 1 slice
Servings per pan: 12
Calories: 133.7
Fat: 2.3g
Sodium: 49mg
Total Carbs: 23g
Fiber: 1g
Protein: 4g

Honey wheat bread recipe

Whole wheat flour is interesting in that it has high protein content, but not a high amount of available gluten. This is because a lot of the bran and germ has been ground into the flour, so these parts of the wheat kernel do not have available gluten. In fact, they prevent gluten chains from tangling with each other. As a result, if you wish to avoid very heavy bread, it can be a good idea to incorporate some bread flour in order to make sure the final loaf will have enough structure to proof.

Equipment
Microwave safe measuring cup
Wooden cutting board
Large work bowl, with cover or plastic wrap
Plastic mixing spoon
Non-stick cooking spray
Standard loaf pan
Board scraper

Ingredients
1 teaspoon of salt
1¼ cups of warm water (approximately 90 degrees Fahrenheit)
2 tablespoons of honey
2 tablespoons of olive oil
2 teaspoons of active dry yeast
1½ cups of bread flour
1½ cups of whole wheat flour

Method
1. Pour the water and honey into a microwave safe mixing cup. Microwave on high for one minute, or until the water reaches a temperature of 90 to 100 degrees Fahrenheit.

2. Stir the water to make sure the honey has dissolved. Then add the yeast and stir until all the granules have dissolved into the water. Set the cup aside for five minutes to allow the yeast to activate and bloom.

3. Add the flour to a large work bowl.

4. Once the yeast has bloomed and formed a frothy head, pour it onto the flour along with the olive oil. Do not add the salt yet!

5. Stir to combine, and then wait five minutes. This additional time will allow the flour to hydrate, and you will have more gluten available when you knead the dough. Whole wheat bread needs a little bit longer to hydrate than bread flour or all-purpose flour.

6. Lightly flour a wooden work surface and turn the dough out. Spray the work bowl with non-stick cooking spray.

7. Begin kneading using the folding technique. Press the dough out into a roughly rectangular shape. Sprinkle a little bit of salt on the east side. Fold the west side over it and press it out into a rectangle. Next, sprinkle a little bit of the salt on the south side of the dough and fold the north side over it. Press it out into a rectangle. Continue folding and sprinkling salt until all of the salt has been used.

8. Once it is sufficiently kneaded, return it to the work bowl. Set your oven to warm for a few minutes. Then wet your hands and rub the surface to wet the dough ball. Cover and place in the warm oven to let the dough proof.

When proofing, the internal temperature of the oven should be around 90 to100 degrees Fahrenheit, and never over 120. Allow the dough to rise in the warm oven until it doubles in size. This generally takes around 45 minutes to an hour.

9. This stage is called punching down the dough. Really, you are coaxing it into the shape of a dough ball so you can form the loaf. While this recipe can make two medium sized loaves, it is arguably better to make one large one.

Turn the dough out onto the counter. Using a board scraper, fold the sides under the main mass of the dough. Lift the mass of the dough ball up and pinch the seams together to form a tight dough ball.

10. Use the non-stick cooking spray to grease the loaf pan. Rewarm the oven again if it needs it.

11. Form the final loaf by rolling the dough back and forth evenly until it is the length of the bread pan. When it is the right size, place it in the pan.

12. Wet your hands, and lightly rub the loaf just enough to dampen the surface. This will help develop a deeper brown crust. Use a paring knife to make three shallow, diagonal slits, which is insurance against the crown collapsing during the final rise.

13. Place the loaf pan back in the warm oven for the final rise. This will take roughly 30 to 45 minutes. Once the loaf rises an inch or two above the lip of the loaf pan, it is ready to bake. Allowing it to proof longer will give you a larger loaf with a fluffy interior. However, if you allow the loaf to proof too much,

the gluten structure of the unbaked crown could fail, and the loaf could potentially collapse.

14. Consider your method for adding steam to the oven. Spraying water from a spray bottle is a common method. However, a small, shallow pan of water placed in the back corner on a lower rack is also an easy option, as you won't lose heat opening the oven door.

15. Bake at 380 degrees Fahrenheit for 30 to 35 minutes, or until the internal temperature of the loaf is 200 degrees Fahrenheit.

16. When the loaf has reached a temperature of 200 degrees Fahrenheit, remove it from the oven. Turn it out of the pan onto a wooden cutting board. You should give the loaf a full hour to cool down. This cooling time will help the crust to set, and the internal steam to redistribute. The end result is a loaf that is much easier to cut.

Honey wheat bread is best served with a honey butter spread made from 1 tablespoon of honey whipped with 4 tablespoons of butter.

Nutrition facts
Serving size: 1 slice
Servings per pan: 12
Calories: 135.6
Fat: 2.4g
Sodium: 51mg
Total Carbs: 24.3g
Fiber: 1.5g
Protein: 4g

Multi-grain wheat bread recipe

We already mentioned the characteristics and challenges of whole wheat flour in the last recipe, but those of multi-grain cereal also need to be considered.

Multi-grain cereal is completely devoid of available gluten, and its large grain size greatly interferes with the formation of gluten chains. One technique that helps is soaking the multi-grain cereal in the warm water for 10 minutes before adding the malted barley syrup. Once the cereal has softened, you can then use the same water to bloom the yeast. This softened cereal is a little easier for gluten to tangle around and it also gives a softer texture to the final bread.

There are many different brands and blends of multi-grain cereal available. Most of them are similar to old fashioned Maypo cereal. It is usually best to start your search in the organic foods aisle of your grocery store.

Equipment
Microwave safe measuring cup
Wooden cutting board
Large work bowl, with cover or plastic wrap
Two small bowls
Plastic mixing spoon
Non-stick cooking spray
Standard loaf pan
Board scraper

Ingredients
1 teaspoon of salt
1¼ cups of warm water (approximately 90 degrees Fahrenheit)

2 tablespoons of malted barley syrup
3 tablespoons of sunflower oil
2 teaspoons of active dry yeast
1½ cups of bread flour
1½ cups of whole wheat flour
¼ cup of cereal blend (preferably 10 grain)
2 tablespoons of quick oatmeal, roughly chopped
2 tablespoons of sunflower seeds, roughly chopped

Method

1. Pour the water and multi-grain cereal into a microwave safe mixing cup. Microwave on high for two minutes, or until the water reaches a temperature of 120 degrees Fahrenheit. Set the cup aside and allow the water to cool down to a temperature of 90 to 100 degrees Fahrenheit.

2. While the water is cooling, chop the sunflower seeds and oatmeal, keeping them in separate small bowls.

3. Once the water cools, add the malted barley syrup to the water. Stir the water to make sure the syrup has dissolved. Then add the yeast and stir until all the granules have dissolved in the water. Set the cup aside for five minutes to allow the yeast to bloom.

4. Add the bread flour, chopped sunflower seeds, and whole wheat flour to a large work bowl.

5. Once the yeast has bloomed and formed a frothy head, pour it onto the flour mixture along with the sunflower oil. Do not add the salt yet!

6. Stir to combine, and wait seven minutes for the whole wheat flour to hydrate.

7. Lightly flour a wooden work surface, and turn the dough out. Spray the work bowl with non-stick cooking spray.

8. Begin kneading and adding salt using the folding technique discussed earlier.

9. Once it is sufficiently kneaded, return the dough to the work bowl. Set your oven to warm for a few minutes. Then wet your hands, and rub the surface to wet the dough ball. Cover, and place in the warm oven to let the dough proof.

10. Allow the dough to rise in the warm oven until the dough doubles in size. This generally takes an hour.

11. This stage is called punching down the dough. Really though you are coaxing it into the shape of a dough ball so you can form the loaf.

Turn the dough out onto the counter. Using a board scraper, fold the sides under the main mass of the dough. Lift the mass of the dough ball up, and pinch the seams together to form a tight dough ball.

12. Use the non-stick cooking spray to grease the loaf pan. Rewarm the oven again if it needs it.

13. Form the final loaf by rolling the dough back and forth evenly until it is the length of the bread pan.

14. Wet your hands, and lightly rub the loaf just enough to dampen the surface. Sprinkle the chopped oatmeal onto a clean surface and gently roll the crown of the bread onto it. This should stick the oatmeal to the crown. Place the dough into the pan, then use a paring knife to make three shallow, diagonal slits across the crown of the loaf.

15. Place the loaf pan back in the warm oven for the final rise. This will take roughly 45 minutes. Once the loaf rises an inch or two above the lip of the loaf pan it is ready to bake.

16. Prepare your preferred method of adding steam.

17. Bake at 380 degrees Fahrenheit for 30 to 35 minutes, or until the internal temperature of the loaf is 200 degrees.

18. When the loaf has reached a temperature of 200 degrees Fahrenheit, remove it from the oven, and turn it out of the pan onto a wooden cutting board.

Nutrition facts
Serving size: 1 slice
Servings per pan: 12
Calories: 172.6
Fat: 4.9g
Sodium: 52mg
Total Carbs: 33.7g
Fiber: 4.5g
Protein: 6.8g

New York-style pizza dough

Being able to make your own pizza at home is not only a healthy alternative to corporate franchise pizza, it is also a great way to save money, it's fun to make as a family, and it's delicious. Sauce, cheese, and topping combinations are limited only by your imagination.

Preparing dough for a New York-style crust starts out very similar to how you make a loaf of white bread. The amount of oil is increased in order to make the crust richer and crisper. Using instant dry yeast will help give you a little bit more of a bubbly crust.

Equipment
Microwave safe measuring cup
Wooden cutting board
Large work bowl, with cover or plastic wrap
Plastic mixing spoon
Non-stick cooking spray
Board scraper
Pizza stone

Ingredients
1 teaspoon of salt
1 cup of warm water (approximately 90 degrees Fahrenheit)
2 tablespoons of sugar
4 tablespoons of olive oil
3 teaspoons of instant dry yeast
3 cups of bread flour
Cornmeal

Method

1. Pour the water and sugar into a microwave safe mixing cup. Microwave on high for one minute, or until the water reaches a temperature of 90 to 100 degrees Fahrenheit.

2. Stir the water to make sure the sugar has dissolved. Then add the yeast and stir until all the granules have dissolved into the water. Set the cup aside for five minutes to allow the yeast to activate and bloom.

3. Add the flour to a large work bowl.

4. Once the yeast has bloomed and formed a frothy head, pour it onto the flour along with the olive oil. Do not add the salt yet!

5. Stir to combine, and then wait five minutes. This additional time will allow the flour to hydrate, and you will have more gluten available when you knead the dough. This will contribute to a nice crispy crust that will help keep the slices from drooping under the weight of toppings and cheese.

6. Lightly flour a wooden work surface and turn the dough out. Spray the work bowl with non-stick cooking spray.

7. Begin kneading using the folding technique. Press the dough out into a roughly rectangular shape.

8. Once it is sufficiently kneaded, return it to the work bowl. Set your oven to warm for a few minutes. Cover, and place in the warm oven to let the dough proof.

When proofing, the internal temperature of the oven should be around 90 to 100 degrees Fahrenheit and never over 120. Allow the dough to rise in the warm oven until it doubles in size. This generally takes around 30 minutes.

9. Turn the dough ball out onto a floured surface and form a tight dough ball. Allow the dough ball to sit for 3 to 5 minutes.

10. Preheat the oven to 450 degrees Fahrenheit.

11. Press the dough ball out into a flat circle. Use a floured rolling pin to spread it out. Make sure you are rolling evenly, alternating between rolling east-west and north-south. You can continue rolling with the rolling pin until you have reached your desired thickness. When rolled thin, this recipe will completely cover most pizza stones. How thick or thin you like your pizza crust is entirely a matter of personal preference.

12. Once it is the desired thickness, place the dough on a pizza stone that has been lightly dusted with cornmeal.

13. Dock the dough by lightly pricking it all over with a fork. This will reduce the chance of large catastrophic bubbles forming during baking.

14. Dress the pizza with sauce, cheese, and toppings of your preference. It is best to go light on the toppings if you want a crust that is crispy in the middle.

15. Place the pizza stone in the oven and bake for 20 minutes or until the outer crust is golden brown.

Nutrition facts
Serving size: 1 slice
Servings per pan: 12

Calories: 153.7
Fat: 4.6g
Sodium: 49mg
Total Carbs: 23g
Fiber: 1g
Protein: 4g

Whole wheat pizza crust

This recipe and procedure is almost the same as the New York-style pizza crust, except that it uses whole wheat flour.

Equipment
Microwave safe measuring cup
Wooden cutting board
Large work bowl, with cover or plastic wrap
Plastic mixing spoon
Non-stick cooking spray
Board scraper
Pizza stone

Ingredients
1¼ teaspoon of salt
1 cup of warm water (approximately 90 degrees Fahrenheit)
1½ tablespoons of malted barley syrup
4 tablespoons of olive oil
3 teaspoons of instant dry yeast
1½ cups of bread flour
1½ cups of whole wheat flour
Cornmeal

Method
Follow the same method as for the New York-style pizza dough.

Nutrition facts
Serving size: 1 slice
Servings per pan: 12
Calories: 135
Fat: 4.6g

Sodium: 51mg
Total Carbs: 23.8g
Fiber: 1.5g
Protein: 4g

Focaccia bread with rosemary

Focaccia bread is soft and rich with a crispy exterior. It typically includes garlic, herbs, and black pepper for flavor. While at home in Mediterranean cuisine, it is also goes down well at a barbecue.

Equipment
Large work bowl with cover or plastic wrap
Plastic mixing spoon
Non-stick spray
Half sheet pan lined with parchment paper
Basting brush
Pizza cutter

Ingredients
3 cups of bread flour
1 teaspoon of salt
1 teaspoon of kosher salt, reserved
3 teaspoons of active dry yeast
6 cloves of garlic, minced
2 tablespoons of fresh oregano, chopped
8 leaves of fresh basil, chopped
3 tablespoons of fresh rosemary, chopped
1½ teaspoons of fresh ground black pepper
3 tablespoons of olive oil
3 tablespoons of olive oil, reserved
1 ½ cups of warm water
½ cup of shredded Asiago cheese

Method

1. Heat the water in a microwave safe mixing cup to a temperature of 90 to 100 degrees. Add the yeast, stir, and allow it to bloom for five minutes.

2. Combine the flour, garlic, herbs, and black pepper in a large work bowl. Stir to combine and evenly distribute the herbs.

3. Pour the yeast and olive oil into the bowl with the dry ingredients. Stir to combine. Wait 5 minutes to let the flour thoroughly hydrate.

4. Begin kneading using the folding technique, sprinkling a little salt with each fold.

5. Spray the work bowl with non-stick cooking spray and place the dough back into the bowl. Cover the bowl, and leave it out at room temperature until it doubles in size.

The ambient room temperature will be a factor in how long it takes for the dough to double in size. You should allow for a one to two hour proofing time. Much like a classic sponge, the longer the dough is allowed to proof, the more flavor will develop.

6. Line a half sheet pan with parchment paper, and grease it lightly with olive oil. Adding the olive oil to the parchment paper will give the final bread a rich, crispy bottom.

7. Spread the dough on the sheet pan, and lightly press it out. Use a basting brush to lightly paint the top of the bread with olive oil.

8. Sprinkle the kosher salt and Asiago cheese over the top.

9. Warm the oven to a temperature between 90 to 100 degrees Fahrenheit, just like you would do in the initial proofing of a basic loaf. Place the sheet pan in the warm oven for twenty minutes until the dough bounces back to roughly double its thickness.

10. Heat the oven to 450 degrees Fahrenheit, with the pan still in the oven. Bake the bread for 13 to 15 minutes, or until the top is golden brown.

11. Use the parchment paper to help slide the bread out of the pan and onto a cutting board. Then slide the parchment paper out from underneath the focaccia.

12. Allow to cool for 10 minutes before cutting it into squares with a pizza cutter.

Nutrition facts
Serving size: 1 square
Servings per pan: 12
Calories: 329
Fat: 23.5
Sodium: 162mg
Total Carbs: 23.8g
Fiber: 1g
Protein: 6.4g

Ciabatta bread

Ciabatta bread is one of the great, classic Italian breads. It utilizes an interesting technique for increasing flavor in the final loaf.

Patience is a virtue, and ciabatta bread is an exercise in patience. When done right, ciabatta bread takes a full 24 hours from the first moment you start measuring the ingredients until you bite down into the crisp crust and relish its soft, tasty interior.

When it comes to flour selection there is a narrow line between all-purpose flour and bread flour. All-purpose flour can work just fine for this recipe, providing it has sufficient protein. However, all-purpose flour can be inconsistent in its protein content. If you were to use all-purpose flour with low protein content, it would make a loaf that spreads out too wide, and fails to rise. So, for the sake of consistency, it's best to make this recipe with bread flour.

Ciabatta bread calls for the creation of a sponge. This is a small batch of dough which is allowed to ferment for up to a day in advance, creating complex earthy flavors in the bread. Proofing at room temperature allows the yeast to contribute gasses and lactic acid to the flour in a way that you usually can only find in wild yeast.

When working with this dough, you have to be mindful that it is very sticky and will require careful handling. It is a good idea to spray your hands with non-stick spray, or use latex gloves before touching the dough.

Equipment
Large work bowl with cover or plastic wrap
Plastic mixing spoon
Parchment paper
Pizza stone
Wooden cutting board

Sponge ingredients
1 cup of bread flour
2 tablespoons of whole wheat flour
½ teaspoon of dry active yeast
½ cup of warm water

Dough ingredients
3 cups of bread flour
1 teaspoon of salt
2 teaspoons of dry active yeast
2 tablespoons of olive oil
1 ¼ cups of warm water
2 tablespoons of whole milk
¼ cup of bread flour, reserved for dusting

Method
1. To create a sponge, bloom the yeast in a small amount of water. Add it to the flour in the large work bowl, then cover the bowl and let it stand overnight at room temperature.

2. Thickly coat a piece of parchment paper with non-stick spray. Remove the sponge from the work bowl and place it on the paper. The sponge will be very sticky. Spraying non-stick spray on your hands or wearing latex gloves will help with handling.

3. Heat the water in a microwave safe measuring cup to a temperature of 90 to 100 degrees. Add the yeast, stir to combine, and allow five minutes for it to bloom.

4. Add the flour, olive oil, and milk to the work bowl. Pour the bloomed yeast and water into the work bowl. Stir to combine. Wait 5 minutes for the flour to hydrate.

5. Heavily flour a wooden cutting board. The dough mixture will also be sticky. Place the dough on the floured cutting board, and lightly press it out into an oval. Lightly sprinkle the salt over the entire oval of dough.

6. Grease the work bowl with olive oil.

7. The kneading technique for ciabatta is slightly different from other breads.

Pick up the sponge, and lay it over the dough. Carefully fold the south end of the dough into the middle. Then fold the north end of the dough into the middle, as if you were folding a letter. Use your knuckles to massage the dough, and sponge together. This should remind you of a cat kneading a pillow.

Continue knuckle kneading for one minute.

8. Once the dough and sponge are married together, use the standard folding technique for kneading. If you are using a stand mixer with a dough hook to knead the dough and sponge together, you will have to stop the mixer 4 to 5 times to peel the dough off the hook. Because the dough is so sticky it tends to climb sooner than traditional dough.

9. Knead for 5 to 7 minutes. Dust more flour on the dough if it proves too sticky.

10. Place the dough back into a covered work bowl at room temperature. Depending on the temperature and relative humidity in the room, the dough should take 45 minutes to an hour to double in size.

11. Place the pizza stone in the oven, and preheat it to 425 degrees Fahrenheit.

12. Line a pizza peel or your wooden cutting board with parchment paper. Lightly flour the parchment paper, and gently turn the dough out onto the pizza stone. It is important to be gentle as there are large gas bubbles inside the dough that you do not want to deflate as you form the loaf.

13. Lightly flour your hands before using your fingers to tuck the sides under the middle. Use two hands at a time on each side of the dough. Each time to you tuck a little bit of the sides under you should lift and stretch to elongate the loaf. By the time you reach the ends you should have a loaf that is modestly longer than it is wide.

14. Wet your hands and gently caress the top of the dough. Allow the dough to spring back any volume that may have been lost by you manipulating it. This may take up to 30 minutes.

15. Open the oven door. Carefully slide the parchment paper off the cutting board, and onto the hot pizza stone.

16. Bake for 25 to 27 minutes or until the loaf is dark golden brown with an internal temperature of 205 degrees Fahrenheit.

17. When taking the loaf out of the oven, it is easier to slide the parchment paper back onto the wooden cutting board and leave the stone in the oven. Allow the loaf to cool for 15 minutes before carefully sliding the parchment paper out from under it.

18. Allow the loaf to cool for one hour so the crust can set before cutting it.

Ciabatta is perfectly at home with any Italian dish. While many Americans will apply butter to a slice of ciabatta, a traditional Italian approach is to use a quality, spicy, extra-virgin olive oil.

Nutrition facts
Serving size: 1 slice
Servings per pan: 12
Calories: 144.5
Fat: 2.3g
Sodium: 50mg
Total Carbs: 25.1g
Fiber: 1.2g
Protein: 4.3g

Sourdough bread

Did you know that the world is actually full of wild yeast? Most have no role in the kitchen, and they go unnoticed or ignored. However, you might find it interesting to know that many regions of the world have their own natural form of baker's yeast living wild in the air.

You have probably heard of San Francisco being one of the great places to get tasty sourdough bread. This is because the wild yeast living around San Francisco happens to produce bread that many people find delicious. At the same time, not every region has a type of wild yeast that makes delicious bread.

As well as harvesting yeast from the air, there are fruits such as organically grown apples and grapes that also have a type of wild yeast growing on the peel or skin that can be captured by adding the untreated skins to a sourdough culture.

The first step in making sourdough bread is to create a sourdough starter or culture. An equal amount of whole wheat flour is essential to making a starter, as whole wheat flour contains more of the nutrients that wild yeast prefer to eat.

All flours need to be unbleached, and water must be non-chlorinated. You are essentially attempting to capture a small number of yeast microbes, and encourage them to reproduce in your flour and water mixture. Since chlorine is very good at killing microbes, any amount of it in the starter culture at any time could lead to failure.

Sourdough starter recipe

Equipment
A glass work bowl with a tight lid
Silicone spatula or stainless steel mixing spoon

Ingredients
2 cups of whole wheat flour
2 cups of unbleached all-purpose flour
4 cups of non-chlorinated water

Method
1. Combine 1 cup of whole wheat flour, 1 cup of all-purpose flour, and 1 cup of water.

2. Cover the mixture and allow it to sit at room temperature for 24 hours.

3. The next day remove half of the mixture, and then add another ½ cup of whole wheat flour, ½ cup of all-purpose flour, along with 1 cup of non-chlorinated water. Stir to combine.

While it might seem wasteful to discard half of the original mixture, it is important to keep offering the infant yeast culture a consistent nutrient load, without simply making a massive amount. If you wanted to make a second starter culture to give to a friend, you could take the amount you removed and repeat the process in a second glass bowl.

4. Every day for the next week you will feed the starter twice daily. Each feeding should be ¼ cup of all-purpose flour and ¼

cup of water. By the end of the third day or the beginning of the fourth, you should see some bubbling and frothing.

5. After this week of double feedings, the starter should be ready to use. It will still require a half cup feeding of flour and water every other day in order to keep the yeast active.

Equipment
Microwave safe measuring cup
Wooden cutting board
Large work bowl, with cover or plastic wrap
Plastic mixing spoon
Non-stick cooking spray
Standard loaf pan
Board scraper

Ingredients
1½ cups of active sourdough starter
2 teaspoons of active dry yeast
1½ cups of warm water
2 teaspoons of sugar
2 teaspoons of salt
4 cups of bread flour

Method
1. Pour the water and sugar into a microwave safe mixing cup. Microwave on high for one minute, or until the water reaches a temperature of 90 to 100 degrees Fahrenheit.

2. Stir the water to make sure the sugar has dissolved. Then add the yeast and stir until all the granules have dissolved into the water. Set the cup aside for five minutes to allow the yeast to bloom.

3. Add the flour and sourdough starter to a large work bowl.

4. Once the yeast has bloomed and formed a frothy head, pour it onto the flour mixture. Do not add the salt yet!

5. Stir to combine, and then wait 5 minutes. This additional time will allow the flour to hydrate, and you will have more gluten available when you knead the dough.

6. Lightly flour a wooden work surface, and turn the dough out. Spray the work bowl with non-stick cooking spray.

7. Begin kneading and adding salt using the folding technique.

8. Once it is sufficiently kneaded, return the dough to the work bowl. Set your oven to warm for a few minutes. Then wet your hands and rub the surface of the dough ball. Cover and place in the warm oven to let the dough proof.

Allow the dough to rise in the warm oven until it doubles in size. This generally takes 45 minutes to an hour.

9. Now you're ready to punch down the dough. Turn the dough out onto the counter. Using a board scraper, fold the sides under the main mass of the dough. Lift the mass of the dough ball up, and pinch the seams together to form a tight dough ball.

10. Use the non-stick cooking spray to grease the loaf pan. Rewarm the oven again if it needs it.

11. Form the final loaf by rolling the dough back and forth until it is the length of the bread pan. When it is the right size, place it in the pan.

12. Wet your hands and lightly rub the loaf just enough to dampen the surface. This will help develop a deeper brown crust. Use a paring knife to make three shallow, diagonal slits across the crown of the loaf.

13. Place the loaf pan back in the warm oven for the final rise. This will take roughly 30 to 45 minutes. Once the loaf rises an inch or two above the lip of the loaf pan, it is ready to bake.

14. Prepare your preferred method of adding steam.

15. Bake at 400 degrees Fahrenheit for 25 to 30 minutes or until the internal temperature of the loaf is 200 degrees.

16. When the loaf has reached a temperature of 200 degrees Fahrenheit, remove it from the oven and turn it out of the pan onto a wooden cutting board.

This bread is excellent for making a wide variety of fresh sandwiches. It can also be toasted or pressed for Panini.

Nutrition facts
Serving size: 1 slice
Servings per pan: 12
Calories: 80
Fat: 1g
Sodium: 180 mg
Total Carbs: 17g
Fiber: 1g
Protein: 3g

Gluten-free and Paleo breads

Two of the fastest growing movements in the world of health and nutrition are gluten-free and Paleo diets. While these are two distinctly different diet programs, they do share a common philosophy that excludes gluten. In fact, all Paleo food is inherently gluten-free. However, not all gluten-free food is necessarily Paleo, because people following the Paleo diet do not eat any grains at all, including rice and others allowed in gluten-free diets.

The gluten-free diet is a response to the growing number of people who have developed Celiac disease. People with Celiac have sensitivity to the gluten compounds found in wheat, which cause the intestinal lining to become inflamed, leading to digestive problems. Additionally, there are others who are not celiacs but still believe that refraining from eating gluten has many health benefits.

People who subscribe to the Paleo diet operate under the philosophy that the diet of our primitive ancestors was much healthier and more nutritious than the modern diet, which includes processed grains.

However, even people following gluten-free and Paleo diets can still enjoy homemade bread. Here are two great recipes to get started – one for gluten-free brioche and another for Paleo bread.

Gluten-free brioche recipe

Traditionally, brioche is a wheat bread made from egg-enriched dough. It is then baked until it has a crispy golden exterior with a tender interior.

In this case we will be using a blend of gluten-free flours. The following ingredients (when combined with two eggs) will create a mixture that roughly replicates all-purpose flour:

2 cups brown rice flour
1 cup tapioca starch
½ cup corn starch
1 tablespoon xanthan gum

The dry ingredients should be combined well. Then store the mix in an air-tight glass container until you need it, either for this recipe or another. Add the two eggs with whatever wet ingredients your recipe calls for. In this case, since brioche calls for more egg protein, we will be adding four total eggs to the recipe in order to bind the mix, as well as provide the hallmark richness of a classical brioche.

Equipment
Large work bowl
Small work bowl
Silicone spatula
Standard 9 inch loaf pan

Ingredients
3½ cups of gluten-free flour blend (see above, or use your own preferred blend)

3 tablespoons of butter, melted
3 tablespoon of dry active yeast
3 tablespoons of honey
½ cup of warm milk
1 teaspoon of salt
4 eggs

Method
1. Pour the water and honey into a microwave safe mixing cup. Microwave on high for one minute, or until the water reaches a temperature of 90 to 100 degrees Fahrenheit.

2. Stir the water to make sure the honey has dissolved. Then add the yeast and stir until all the granules have dissolved into the water. Set the cup aside for five minutes, to allow the yeast to bloom.

3. Add the flour blend and salt to a large work bowl.

4. Once the yeast has bloomed and formed a frothy head, pour it onto the flour mixture along with the milk and melted butter.

5. Beat the 4 eggs in a small work bowl before adding them to the mixture.

6. Stir to combine, and then wait 5 minutes. This additional time will allow the dry ingredients to hydrate.

7. Because gluten-free mixes create looser, wetter batters rather than firmer doughs, you will not knead this recipe. Simply cover the bowl and place in a pre-warmed oven (90-100 degrees Fahrenheit) to proof until it doubles in size. This generally takes 45 minutes to an hour.

8. Use the non-stick cooking spray to grease the loaf pan.

9. Scrape the brioche mix into the pan, then put the loaf pan back in the warm oven for the final rise. This will take roughly 30 to 45 minutes. Once the loaf rises an inch or two above the lip of the loaf pan, it is ready to bake. Note this recipe does not call for the addition of steam like you would normally use when baking a loaf of bread made from wheat flour.

10. Bake at 400 degrees Fahrenheit for 25 to 30 minutes, or until a toothpick inserted into the center comes out clean

11. Remove it from the oven and turn it out of the pan onto a wooden cutting board.

Nutrition facts
Serving size: 1 slice
Servings per pan: 12
Calories: 184
Fat: 3.9g
Sodium: 200.5 mg
Total Carbs: 56.7g
Fiber: 23.4g
Protein: 2.1g

Paleo bread

This is a recipe for a simple loaf of bread made using almond flour and coconut flour. The bread is leavened by baking soda, and is somewhat similar to beer bread. Except, of course, it does not call for beer!

Equipment
Food processor
Small work bowl
Large work bowl
Silicone spatula
Standard loaf pan

Ingredients
1½ cups of blanched almond flour
2 tablespoons of coconut flour
1¼ cup of flaxseed
½ teaspoon of sea salt
1½ teaspoons of baking soda
3 eggs
¼ cup of coconut oil
2 tablespoons of raw honey
2 tablespoons of apple cider vinegar

Method
1. Preheat the oven to 375 degrees, and grease a standard 9 inch loaf pan with oil.

2. Add the flaxseed to the work bowl of your food processor and pulse 7 to 10 times to create a flaxseed meal. This will give the bread a mild grain texture, while the flaxseed contributes healthy oils to the dough.

3. Add the almond flour, coconut flour, baking soda, and sea salt to the food processor. Then pulse 5 to 7 times to combine.

4. Beat the eggs in a small work bowl. Then slowly pour them into the food processor through the feeder chute. Pulse periodically to make sure it is incorporating evenly. The goal is to avoid egg wads clumping in the flour!

5. Use the same slow pour method to incorporate the oil, honey, and vinegar.

6. Pour the batter into the greased loaf pan. Shake the pan back and forth to make sure the it levels.

7. Place the pan into the preheated oven and bake for 30 to 35 minutes, or until a toothpick inserted into the middle comes out clean.

8. Turn the loaf out onto a wooden cutting board. Allow the loaf to cool for 30 minutes before slicing.

Nutrition facts
Serving size: 1 slice
Servings per pan: 12
Calories: 125
Fat: 10g
Sodium: 300 mg
Total Carbs: 3.6g
Fiber: 2.2g
Protein: 4.4g

Conclusion

Making your own bread at home is not only a great way to feed your family healthy and nutritious bread, it is also a great way to save money. Apart from that, there's something immensely satisfying in knowing that you made something so delicious yourself. Trust me – your friends and family will love it!

Now that you have all the basic knowledge in this book under your belt, you're truly equipped to start your journey into the world of homemade bread baking.

I hope it will be as rewarding and fulfilling a journey as mine.

9 781495 940057